PREFACE

The Cooperative Quilt

By Lon McClintock, President, PeaceQuilts Board of Directors

Quilting is both a solitary and a social activity. It provides a time to work alone, in quiet, and a time to work with friends, in conversation. It is both craft and art. One cannot tell if a quilter experiences greater joy looking over a freshly finished quilt, or laying out freshly pressed fabrics for a piece to be created.

What is striking about the tradition of quilting is that it draws people together, to work, to encourage one another, and to enjoy what they create. And so it has been with PeaceQuilts. Quilting traditions have served as a model for the Haitian women whose work appears in the pages of this catalog. These women and their work, in turn, have inspired a much larger collaboration of volunteers and supporter, both in Haiti and the United States.

PeaceQuilts began as an idea to teach Haitian women a marketable skill, one that could provide an income to support the quilters and their families. It has now become a non-profit, all-volunteer humanitarian organization that assists in the development of quilting cooperatives in Haiti. PeaceQuilts' volunteers raise funds, collect quilting materials and supplies, and provide direct training and support to cooperative members in Haiti. The goal is to nurture these cooperatives until they are self-directed and self-sustaining. All proceeds from the sale of the quilts go directly to the quilters and to further the work of PeaceQuilts to relieve poverty in Haiti.

To learn more about PeaceQuilts and how you can help, or to purchase one of these beautiful, original art quilts, visit: www.haitipeacequilts.org.

Some of the PeaceQuilts volunteers with Sr. Irma, Principal of College Marie Reine Immaculée in Lilavois, Haiti: (from left to right starting in front) Karen Flynn, Betsy Marshall, Jeanne Staples, Jo Van Loo, Maureen Matthews McClintock, Sr. Irma, Tomar Waldman

Aerial photo of Haiti showing an example of the widespread deforestation which affects the country's agricultural and fishing industries, and contributes to the devastating effects of tropical storms and hurricanes. Haiti's primary cooking fuel is charcoal. *Photo courtesy of Eric Anderson*

*Di m'ki sa ou renmen,
m'a di ou ki moun ou ye.*

Tell me what you love, and I'll tell you who you are.

Haitian proverb

Working on the quilt frame.

PATIENCE TO RAISE THE SUN

Art Quilts from Haiti
& *their Power to Change Women's Lives*

Introduction: Stephen Perkins

■

Essays: Jamie Franklin and Nora Nevin

■

Photographs: Harvey John Beth

CONTENTS

Artisanat Patchwork de Paix, The PeaceQuilts Cooperative in Lilavois, Haiti

Se Bondye sèl ki konn doulè malere.

Only God knows the pain of the poor.

Haitian proverb

INTRODUCTION

By Stephen Perkins, Director, Bennington Museum

L'Union Fait Force – Unity Makes Strength. The Haitian motto, with its French democratic over-tones, can be applied to the workshops that make up the PeaceQuilts program in rural Haiti. Groups of women, and even some men, working together to draw on their rich decorative traditions to create art quilts for the American market creates a living wage for residents of the Western Hemisphere's poorest nation. The extraordinary stories of these people's lives are told through the pages of this book and the sumptuous exhibition *Patience to Raise the Sun.*

How did a museum in rural Vermont discover this program and come to mount a traveling exhibition? The genesis relates back to a Rotary presentation and subsequent sales meeting with the Quilting Coordinator for PeaceQuilts and Bennington County resident, Maureen Mat-thews McClintock, about sales of Haitian quilts in the museum shop. As these incredible quilts emerged from the bag, we quickly saw that these objects and their attendant stories were much too exceptional for a simple display in the museum store.

With their rich embroidery and pictorial imagery, the quilts we viewed that day brought to mind African-American story quilts, yet with a tropical flair and New England construction. The folk art aspect of these works allows the viewer to enter the world of the artist in a way often re-served for more traditional art forms such as painting and sculpture. In a very rare moment for an established museum, we committed to mounting an exhibition of these quilts on the spot.

The Bennington Museum's extensive quilt collection and the strong tradition of quilting in northern New England draw many people to our galleries for our annual fall quilt displays. With Bennington quilters training the Haitian quilters, we saw a unique opportunity for a meaningful exhibition that connects the Bennington region with the broader world community. Thanks to the vision of the PeaceQuilts organization and its Director Jeanne Staples, this one venue show has now been developed into a nationwide traveling exhibition and this beautiful catalogue.

As you read this catalog and reflect on the imagery of the exhibition, the compelling stories of the quilters, and the historical and cultural setting of these works of art, I hope you are inspired to participate in similar programs, be they domestic or international, that make life more full for your neighbors.

*Fòk ou gen pasyans
pou ou leve solèy.*

It takes patience
to raise the sun.

Haitian proverb

PA PALE SA OU PA WE AK PROP ZYE OU.
Never talk about anything you don't see with your own eyes.

Figure 1 – Student embroidery sampler. Quilting and embroidery are part of the sewing curriculum at several training centers for young women. Top graduates can be eligible for membership in a PeaceQuilts' cooperative.

By Jamie Franklin, Curator of Collections, Bennington Museum

Introduction

Located in the Caribbean Sea, in a tropical climate where the temperature rarely drops below 60 degrees Fahrenheit, Haiti understandably has no indigenous quilting tradition. That was until a few years ago, when students at the Centre Menager, a job-training program run by the College Marie Reine Immaculée in Lilavois, began making the colorful, elaborately quilted textiles that are the subject of this catalog and attendant exhibition. It didn't take long for the students to catch on. They quickly soaked in traditional Anglo-American, African-American and African textile/quilting techniques and styles and combined them with their own uniquely Haitian sensibility to create a new and exciting art form. (fig. 1, Embroidery sampler created as training exercise) Haitian women have a deeply rooted tradition of making elaborately embroidered textiles, including articles such as shirts, table cloths, and skirts made for a once booming tourist market and brilliantly sequined flags, known as drapo, originally used to attract Iwa, or spirits, to Vodou ceremonies. Women typically learn embroidery at a young age in Haiti, a skill passed from mother to daughter in small villages throughout the country.

Paintings for sale on a street in Port-au-Prince.

From vibrantly painted murals and hand painted shop signs to brilliantly decorated taxis and buses, Haitians surround themselves with art. Photos courtesy of Tomar Waldman

In addition to widespread embroidery skills amongst its female population, Haiti has a rich artistic and cultural heritage upon which to draw from in creating these quilts. Despite often bleak living conditions, or perhaps as a means to escape them, Haiti is filled with colorful examples of intuitive artistic expression nearly everywhere one looks. From vibrantly painted murals and hand painted shop signs to brilliantly decorated taxis and buses, Haitians surround themselves with art. These typically aren't refined works of art made by trained artists, but rather the product of an honest, unaffected outpouring of creativity that abounds amongst the Haitian people. In 1944 self-taught Haitian

Haitian women have a deeply rooted tradition of making elaborately embroidered textiles, including articles such as shirts, table cloths, and skirts made for a once booming tourist market.

Figure 2 – Vie de Lilavois (Lilavois Life) was the first quilt executed by students studying couture (sewing) at the Centre Menager in Lilavois under the auspices of PeaceQuilts.

Figure 3 and 4 – Vie de Lilavois (details)

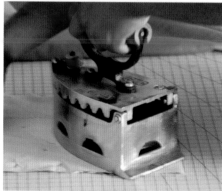

In the absence of electricity, charcoal irons and treadle sewing machines are utilized.

art was "discovered" by the Western art world when the Cuban-born painter Wilfredo Lam, then living in Paris, and the Surrealist artist André Breton visited the recently established Centre d'Art in Haiti's capital, Port-au-Prince. Breton told Dewitt Peters, an American artist who founded the Centre d'Art after traveling to Haiti on a wartime assignment to teach English, that the work he saw "should revolutionize modern painting." After purchasing five works by the Haitian artist Hector Hyppolite, Breton returned with them to Paris where they were enthusiastically received. With a new market for their work there began a renaissance, an explosion of creativity amongst self-taught Haitian artists. In the intervening sixty-five years art has become a defining characteristic of the island nation, widely recognized throughout the world for its vibrant, unhackneyed vision of Haitian life and culture.

(fig. 2) *Vie de Lilavois* ("Lilavois Life") was the first quilt executed by students studying couture (sewing) at the Centre Menager under the auspices of PeaceQuilts. Started, and largely completed, in January 2006 during the first quilting workshop conducted by PeaceQuilts' founder Jeanne Staples, it is, quite possibly, the first quilt ever made in Haiti. To accommodate a workshop with multiple students the quilt was modeled after the sampler or album style quilt, a format popular in America during the mid-nineteenth century, with each block composed of a different design. Accordingly, each young woman in the class worked on her own block, starting with a sketch for the appliqué design, then piecing the corner blocks and sashing. This work was all done by hand, without the aid of a sewing machine, because, as in much of Haiti, there is no electricity at the school in Lilavois. Today, the women often make use of a foot-powered treadle sewing machine to piece their quilts; and for ironing they use irons heated by coals kept hot in a metal brazier. In spite of less than ideal conditions and low-tech methods, the women at PeaceQuilts create works of art that rise above the circumstances in which they are made. Several blocks in *Vie de Lilavois* that were not completely finished at the first workshop were brought back with Staples to the United States, where a group of quilters at the Oak Bluffs Senior Center in Martha's Vineyard, Massachusetts finished what little remained, and then joined the blocks together. In January of 2008, exactly two years later, Staples brought the quilt back to Haiti where the women in the then well-established PeaceQuilts atelier (several of whom had been in the previous group of students) added the binding, label, and slip sleeve. This type of collaboration is illustrative of the hybrid/creolized nature of Haitian art and culture in general.

The imagery used in *Vie de Lilavois* – such as the stylized fruit, flowers, and palm trees –is drawn directly from the quilters' immediate surroundings. Lilavois is a small rural town located northeast

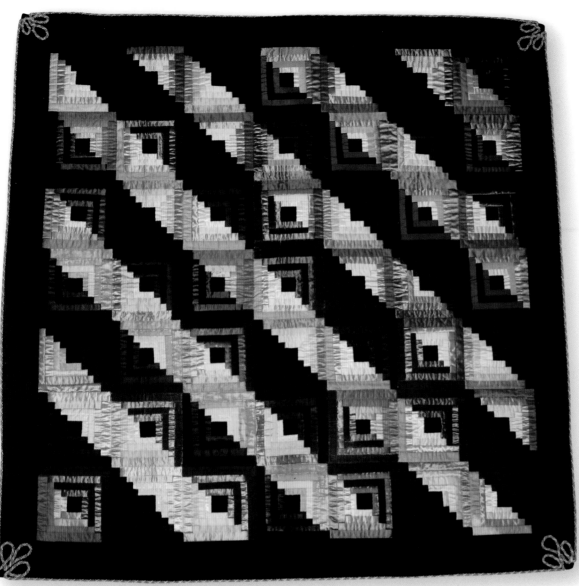

Figure 5 – The Log Cabin, Bennington Museum Collection.

of Haiti's capital city, Port-au-Prince, in a region known as la Plaine du Cul-de-Sac. In a country named after its mountainous terrain (*Haiti* is derived from the indigenous Taino word *Ayiti*, meaning "land on high"), which has been largely deforested and grossly affected by concomitant soil erosion, Plaine du Cul-de-Sac is noted as a fertile valley well recognized for its agriculture and as home to some of Haiti's rare old growth tropical forests. As a result of these lush surroundings, vibrantly colored flowers, fruit, and fruit vendors feature prominently in this and other PeaceQuilts. Two significant blocks (figs. 3 and 4) in *Vie de Lilavois* draw attention to the quilters' deeply felt connection with and pride for their native land. One depicts a variation on the Haitian flag, with a stylized version of the country's seal, featuring crossed banners, a palm tree topped by a liberty cap, and the motto *L'Union Fait Force* ("Unity Makes Strength") embroidered on a background of red and blue. The other distinctive block depicts an idyllic thatch-roofed hut surrounded by embroidered flowers and the phrase *Haiti Cherie* ("My Dear Haiti"), the title of a traditional patriotic song considered by many to be an unofficial national anthem. What truly distinguishes *Vie de Lilavois*, and ultimately all the quilts made by the women in Haiti, is the constant focus on themes and imagery drawn from the

Ranje kabann ou avan domi non je-w.

Put your bed in order before getting sleepy.

Haitian proverb

Figure 6 – *Piti Piti (Little by Little)*   Figure 7 – *Ombre Pete Lumière (Shadows of Light)*

*Sa ou genyen, se li ou
pote nan mache.*

What you have
is what you
bring to the
marketplace.

Haitian proverb

quilters' daily experience and the makers' pride in their country's unique culture. This is in accord with the popular Creole proverb: *Pa pale sa ou pa we ak prop zye ou* - Never talk about anything you don't see with your own eyes.

Genesis of a Craft Tradition

Piti piti zwazo fè nich. –" Little by little, the bird makes his nest."

The quilts made by the women in Lilavois provide us with a unique opportunity to study the genesis of a craft tradition and better understand how such traditions are forged and develop over time. Since quilts are completely foreign to Haiti the women at PeaceQuilts have had to study and learn the art and craft of quilting from the ground up. One way in which they have learned to make and design quilts is by looking at printed images of traditional Anglo- and African-American quilts and African textiles in books and magazines. They have also learned techniques directly from skilled American quilters. This training is carried out under the direction of Maureen Matthews McClintock, PeaceQuilts' quilting coordinator. Haiti has historically been a melting pot of various cultures – African, Spanish, French, etc. – thus the melding of diverse traditions, or creolization, is actually a defining characteristic of their cultural products. Education in Haiti is often by the rote method and imagination is not always encouraged. The instructors of PeaceQuilts have worked closely with the women in the cooperative to develop their intuitive creativity and a sense of personal style. As a result of this encouragement the Haitian quilters have been able to do much more than simply copy quilts out of books. They have taken many traditional Anglo- and African-American quilt designs and made them distinctively their own. To see how the Haitian women have borrowed and adapted from these Anglo- and African-American quilts, as well as African textiles, it will be helpful to compare some of the Haitian quilts to textiles of the type the quilters have studied.

(fig. 5, Benn Mus. Log Cabin) The Log Cabin design is ancient in origin, having been used in Roman tile work and Egyptian mummy wrappings, but it was particularly popular amongst Anglo-American quilt makers during the second half of the nineteenth century and frequently adopted by African-Americans during the twentieth century. The basic Log Cabin quilt block is composed of strips of fabric arranged into triangular quadrants around a central square piece of fabric. The fabrics used can be arranged innumerable ways, with particular attention paid to the contrasts between the relative light and dark values used within each quadrant and overall, so that a myriad of small and large scale patterns can be created. A Log Cabin quilt made in the northeastern United States and dating from 1889 in the Bennington Museum collection serves as an example of a traditional Anglo-American approach to the style, the quadrants and blocks carefully laid out so that the lights and darks form an overall design of bold diagonal stripes, a pattern known as *Straight Furrows*. (fig. 6) A Haitian quilt titled *Piti Piti* ("Little by Little") - a name derived from the popular Haitian proverb *Piti piti zwazo fè nich.* ("Little by little, the bird makes his nest.") - serves as an excellent example of how Haitian women have taken a traditional Anglo/African-American quilt pattern, in this case a variation on a Log Cabin pattern known as *Court House Steps*, and made it their own. This quilt was likely modeled after an African-American quilt in the Log Cabin pattern, as it features many elements, as do many of the PeaceQuilts, that closely relate to African-American quilting traditions, which them-selves relate back to textile traditions brought over the Atlantic from Africa by slaves in the 17th and 18th centuries. This continuity of textile styles and techniques from Africa to the Americas and now Haiti, is not a direct, conscious carry-over in most cases, but it comes as no surprise, considering that approximately ninety-five percent of Haitians can trace their heritage back to slaves who came from West Africa. Since the women at PeaceQuilts have studied images of African-American quilts and African textiles it is difficult to know if this relationship is simply a matter of them copying/ adapting, or whether these similarities may have deeper, less obvious roots. *Piti Piti* is similar in many respects to African-American quilting in its unorthodox use of color, improvised selection of non-matching fabrics and the slightly off-kilter piecing of inconsistently sized swatches of fabric. Another distinctly non-Anglo element of this quilt's design is the addition of buttons, placed intermittently across the quilt's surface. Traditional African and Haitian textiles, such as Haitian Vodou flags known as *drapo*, often feature surfaces elaborately embellished with sequins, buttons or other three-dimensional ob-jects, such as amulets or even rocks. These three-dimensional additions to the textile surface were originally thought to attract good spirits and/or have talismanic properties that deterred evil spirits. While this original function is likely no longer in the minds of contemporary Haitian quilters, the presence of the buttons is a definite decorative holdover from this originally functional practice.

Figure 8 – Dezobeysans de Jonas (The Disobedience of Jonah)

(fig.7) *Ombre Pete Lumiere* ("Shadows of Light") is another Haitian quilt based on a traditional Log Cabin quilt, this time in the *Barn Raising* pattern. In this example the Haitian quilter has foregone creating intricately pieced Log Cabin blocks from small strips of fabric and simply adapted the large scale *Barn Raising* pattern, composed of alternating dark squares within light squares set on edge, and constructed it out of small blocks and triangles of solid fabric colors pieced together. This may have been a conscious choice on the part of the quilter, as it allows for greater flexibility with color selection, or it may be the result of the quilter basing her design on an illustration in a book where the individual Log Cabin blocks were not easily visible so the quilter was simply adapting the overall design. Like *Piti Piti* this quilt also features some African-American stylistic traits, most notably the improvised color selection. While there is a clear organization of the light and dark fabrics into the *Barn Raising* design and a roughly systematic layout to the individual blocks of color, the quilter wasn't bound to this system and improvised at will.

Developing a Unique Vision - Figurative Appliqué Quilts
Sa ou genyen, Se li ou pote nan mache. ("What you have is what you bring to the marketplace.")

In addition to adapting typical geometrically pieced Anglo- and African-American quilt designs the women at the PeaceQuilts cooperative have developed a distinctive repertoire of figurative appli-qué quilts that are inspired by biblical stories, traditional Haitian proverbs and everyday Haitian

Dezobeysans de Jonas (The Disobedience of Jonah) detail

Figure 9 – l'Arbre de Vie (Tree of Life)

Figure 10 – Tree of Life metalwork silhouette. Metal silhouettes cut from a steel oil barrel – a craft that began in Haiti in the mid twentieth century.

life. Quilts that use figural elements in a narrative or illustrative manner, as opposed to being purely decorative, are relatively uncommon throughout the history of quilting. Possible sources of inspiration for the Haitian quilters include a tradition of story quilts made by African-Americans and album quilts featuring figurative appliqué designs popular in America during the middle of the nineteenth century. Though Haiti is probably best known for its Vodou religion, which is a synthesis of Roman Catholicism and Western African traditions, Catholic influence is in much greater evidence in these quilts. The strong presence of Christian imagery is undoubtedly due to the fact that the first women making quilts in Haiti were educated at a Catholic school, Les Filles de Marie Reine Immaculée, which now serves as the PeaceQuilt atelier's home base. (fig. 8) *Dezobeysans de Jonas* ("The Disobedience of Jonah") illustrates an episode from the popular biblical story of "Jonah and the Whale." The quilt takes this well-known tale and makes it uniquely Haitian – from Jonah's unmistakably Afro-Caribbean visage to the elaborately quilted surface. A propensity towards dense quilting is a distinctive element of many PeaceQuilts, undoubtedly resulting from Haiti's rich tradition of embroidery. The quilt's imagery is based on a silk scarf made by women at another craft atelier similar to PeaceQuilts in Matènwa, Haiti using a unique dye-resist technique. This borrowing of motifs from other Haitian craft traditions serves as a means of perpetuating a distinctive national craft style. (fig. 9) *L'Arbre de Vie* ("Tree of Life") is another quilt whose imagery is directly derived from another, more traditional, Haitian craft. (fig. 10) Artists in Croix des Bouquets, of which Lilavois is a suburb, have been creating metal sculptures from recycled steel oil drums since the mid-twentieth century, a practice made popular through the work of blacksmith Georges Liautaud after his "discovery" by Dewitt Peters in 1955. The designs for these sculptures are first drawn in pencil on paper and then transferred to flattened oil barrels with chalk and cut out with shears and chisels. The sculptures' flat, silhouette format makes them ideal for adapting to appliquéd quilt designs.

Figure 11 – Asafo flag
Kweku Kakanu, born ca. 1910
Fante peoples
Ghana
ca. 1935
Commercial cotton cloth
H x W: 108 x 152.4 cm (42 1/2 x 60 in.)
Museum purchase
88-10-1
Photograph by Franko Khoury
National Museum of African Art
Smithsonian Institution

The choice to illustrate the story of "Jonah and the Whale," with its cautionary message of obedience, undoubtedly relates to Haiti's deeply rooted tradition of instructive and often moralizing proverbs. Though every culture uses proverbs, Haiti is especially rich in them, a practice that is undoubtedly carried over from its Western African heritage. In a largely illiterate country – the nation's literacy rate hovers around 50% - wisdom is passed on orally. In Haiti, proverbs are more than pithy insights. Rather, they play a central role in society, often arbitrating complex social dynamics and even helping to settle court cases. Thus, it should come as no surprise that proverbs have served as a rich source of inspiration for the Haitian quilters in Lilavois. (fig. 11, Smithsonian Flag) A tradition of appliqué banners and flags indigenous to a region in West Africa now occupied by the modern nations of Ghana and Benin is a likely source of inspiration for the use of figurative appliqué to illustrate proverbs. Flags made by the Fante people, natives of modern day Ghana, as emblems of Asafo companies – tribal military organizations that date back to the 1400s – seem to be closely related to the appliqué proverb quilts being made in Haiti, consciously or not. The flags, such as fig. 11, typically illustrate traditional West African proverbs relating to power and authority - in this case "Fish grow fat for the benefit of the crocodile."

In the early stages of the PeaceQuilts cooperative the Haitian women would often name a quilt after a popular Haitian proverb though the quilt's imagery had little or no relation to the proverb's content. (fig.12) *Ranje Kabann ou Avan Domi Non Je-w* ("Make Your Bed Before You Get Sleepy") was created in January of 2007 in a similar manner to *Vie de Lilavois*, with each block created by a different student at Marie Reine Immaculée. The overall theme of nighttime, with the black background fabric and embroidered stars, relates to the concept of bedtime and sleeping, but is not a direct illustration of the proverb. The closest we get to a true illustration in this quilt is the block in the upper

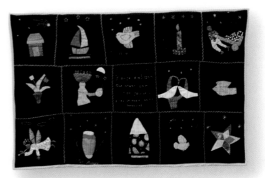

Figure 12 – Ranje Kabann ou Avan Domi Non Je-w
("Make Your Bed Before You Get Sleepy")

*Figure 13 – Dèyè mon gen mon
(Beyond Mountains there are Mountains)*

*Figure 14 – Sa ou genyen, Se li ou Pote nan maché
(What You Have is What You Bring to the Marketplace)*

Figure 15 – Lap Péché Pwason (Fisherman)

Figure 16 – Machann Fwi (Fruit Vendor)

right corner showing a man hauling bones with a hand truck, or putting things in order, which could be an allusion to the proverb's lesson to prepare for the future. *Piti Piti* ("Little by Little"), which was discussed earlier, is another example of a quilt named after a popular Haitian proverb - *Piti piti zwazo fè nich.* ("Little by little, the bird makes his nest.)" - that seems to have little or no relation to the proverb's content. As it is a geometrically pieced, non-figurative quilt, it is hard to imagine how this could be an illustration of a proverb. Yet the naming of *Piti Piti* may have more meaning than it appears at first sight. African-American quilters often give quilt patterns names that relate to their own lives or apply narrative meaning to non-figurative quilts. It seems likely that this could be the case with Piti Piti, as the off-kilter piecing of inconsistently sized swatches of fabric in the quilt – a technique used in many African-American quilts - could easily be interpreted as representing haphazardly constructed birds' nests.

(fig. 13) *Dèyè mòn gen mòn* ("Beyond Mountains there are Mountains") is an excellent example of a more recent quilt by the women in Lilavois that uses a pictorial narrative specifically designed to explicitly illustrate a popular proverb. An exquisitely crafted textile, almost a painting in fabric, this quilt clearly and successfully illustrates a rather abstract concept. With his back to the viewer, a Haitian peasant with a knapsack over his shoulder diligently walks along a road towards a range of mountains in the distance. This image poetically conveys the proverb's lesson that there will be many obstacles to face and one must have the persistence and perseverance to overcome them. (fig. 14) *Sa ou genyen, Se li ou pote nan mache* ("What you have is what you bring to the marketplace") is another proverb quilt, depicting a Haitian woman and her donkey carrying overflowing baskets of fruit to the local market. Like many Haitian proverbs, or idiomatic expressions in any language, the meaning of this saying is somewhat oblique. The lesson of this proverb is that you can only offer that which you have or, in another context, what you see is what you get. The quilts in this book and on display in Patience to Raise the Sun follow this lesson perfectly. Drawing on scenes and experiences from their everyday lives, (figs. 15 and 16) in quilts such as *Lap Péché Pwason* ("Fisherman") and *Machann Fwi* ("Fruit Vendor"), the women at the quilt atelier in Lilavois have created a window into Haitian life.

SA OU PLANTE SE SA OU REKOLTE.

What you plant is what you harvest.

From seeds to Harvest.
The PeaceQuilts Initiative, and How It Grew.

By Nora Nevin

Visit Haiti and you are overwhelmed with impressions: the blinding glare of the sun, the weight of tropical heat, the thin, acrid smell of charcoal fires; the heavily armed guards at gas stations and supermarkets; the small tin-roofed buildings, their concrete blocks held together by oozing and crumbling cement; the ceaseless noises of the night, from Vodou chants to the call-and-response of roosters; trucks constantly braking and shifting gears on the steep slopes and hairpin corners of Port-au-Prince's rutted, once-paved roads.

You will be struck by the people: the beribboned and beaded six-year-olds in their immaculate uniforms on their way to school; those unflappable truck drivers and their laid-back good humor as each competes for his chunk of the road; the handsome and fit young people idly hanging out on the streets, or hanging off the crowded, boisterously illustrated tap-taps, the jitneys that lurch down Haiti's red dust roads.

And you will remember the first woman you meet, Sister Cadet perhaps, a member of the order of *Les Filles de Marie Reine Immaculée,* Daughters of Mary Queen Immaculate, from the *College Ste. Marie.* It is she who will part the oceans of arm-waving porters at the airport, choose two or four, instruct

Dezobeysans de Jonas (The Disobedience of Jonah)
detail

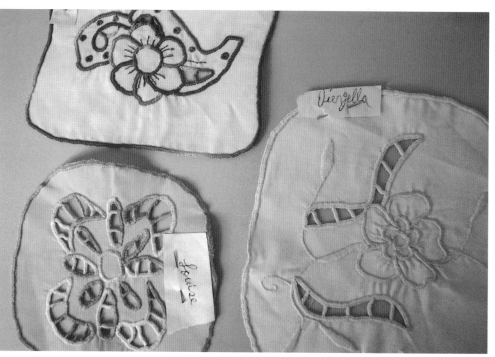

Fancy embroidered cutwork doilies created by students at the Centre Menager (training school).

Sa ki fè pwomès bliey,
sa k'ap espere sonje.

Those who
make promises
forget, those
who are hoping
remember.

Haitian proverb

them in loading your four or twenty pieces of luggage in the back of a battered pickup, direct you to take your place in the cab, pay off the porters keening for more dollars, and hoist herself onto the payload. You will check on her occasionally, and find her saying her rosary beads.

It was because of strong, capable women like Sr. Cadet that Jeanne Staples, founder and director of PeaceQuilts, made her first inquiries about quiltmaking to Sister Gibbs, head of the of the order, and overseer of ten schools and five domestic arts schools known as *Centres Menager,* including the one at Ste. Marie in Port-au-Prince. She knew that the purpose of these schools is to teach young Haitian women skills that would make them make a living: needlework, dressmaking and cooking. Even in Haiti, the most economically depressed nation in the Western hemisphere, the teaching sisters have been determined to make their students eligible for the few jobs available to them in private households, hospitals, and whatever industries might eventually develop. Jeanne knew that in a country where the majority of the population is Catholic, it would be an advantage to have the support of the Church, one of its few stable organizations. In a society traditionally male dominated, it is the women of the Church who are among the most respected for their education, hard work and authority. Their blue-and-white coifs and no-nonsense blue habits have the power to frighten bullies and deflate the pompous.

Jeanne's first trip to the *College Ste. Marie* in Port-au-Prince in January 2006 sprang from frustration. She traveled with Margaret Pénicaud, president and founder of the Martha's Vineyard Fish Farm for Haiti project, whose volunteers hold an annual Haitian art sale each summer. The two women had admired the exquisitely worked table linens volunteers had brought back, along with paintings, sculpture and metal work. They had seen the art and the metal work sell, and sell handsomely. The table linens did not. No one uses table cloths any more, especially the exquisitely embroidered, and no one displays a napkin on a wall. But Jeanne, a professional artist educated at the Pennsylvania Academy of the Fine Arts, knew they were art. How, she wondered, could such beautiful needlework be turned into art that would sell?

Quilting was her answer. Jeanne had grown up with quilts. She and her mother and grandparents collected and used quilts from their native Nova Scotia. She had seen the Quilts of Gees Bend exhibition and been impressed that a pocket of otherwise unsophisticated African American women in rural Alabama had been making highly original, functional quilts for generations, and that a major art institution, the Museum of Fine Arts in Houston, had underwritten an exhibit and an impressive catalog to accompany it. If Gees Bend Quilts could become a genre, why not the Quilts of Haiti?

To be electrified by a vision is one thing; winning over Sr. Gibbs was quite another. No matter that Jeanne was fairly certain that Haitian quilts could become marketable, she knew that a course in quilting had to make sense for the school. She was surprised when Sr. Gibbs agreed to the workshop. "Once she saw quilting as a skill with employment value, it was not a hard sell," said Jeanne. In fact it became "a respectful collaboration." Sr. Gibbs agreed to let her take over two sewing classes, a first-year and a second-year class, more than thirty-five students, at the *Centre Menager* in Lilavois, where the Fish Farm project is located, for one week.

Unable to find a quilter willing to accompany her to Haiti, Jeanne had to learn to quilt. She enlisted several local master quilters on Martha's Vineyard to teach her the fundamentals. In the months that followed, working under the auspices of the Fish Farm Project, Jeanne not only learned how to quilt, but with the help of volunteers, local churches, quilt guilds and the New England Quilt Museum, amassed paper, crayons, colored pencils, fabrics, thread, batting and all manner of teaching supplies. During the course of this trip she and the other volunteers would embark on a teaching mission unlike any they had ever imagined.

One of their first discoveries was that their students seemed to have little experience with crayons, or with drawing a picture. So the volunteers had them draw. They passed out white paper, cut to quilt-square size, and pencils. Some of the students drew images like those on the art show tablecloths: tiny figures, always the same, closely copied. Or palm trees. Or sail boats. Or Mickey Mouse.

PeaceQuilts gets its start under the auspices of the Martha's Vineyard Fish Farm for Haiti Project. Traveling to Haiti in January 2007 are: (From left to right) Jeanne Staples, Karen Flynn, Margaret Pénicaud (Fish Farm founder and Director), and Margaret Spokus.

Sa ou plante se sa ou rekòlte.

What you plant is what you harvest.

Haitian proverb

Students at the Centre Manager (training school) in Lilavois create Vie de Lilavois, the first Haitian quilt.

Master quilter Jo Van Loo (left), assisted by Betsy Marshall (rear right) and Karen Flynn (not pictured) teaches the limitless possibilities of pattern design and the related mathematical concepts with Pattern Blocks.

Noémie Estimé applies mathematical principles of design in a quilting workshop conducted by Jo Van Loo.

Yon pitit ka gen anpil papa men yon sèl manman.

A child can have many fathers, but can have only one mother.

Haitian proverb

"What else?" Jeanne prodded them. "They expected us to tell them what to draw."

Next they were given colored pencils. Jeanne asked them to think about what they saw every day – wildly painted *taptaps*, fruit, flowers, the sun – and draw those. "They loved this part," she said. And after a while they began to draw their own designs.

Her third exercise was to break images into their component parts, perhaps a flower into petal, eye, stem, leaf. Some of the advanced students had learned to appliqué in their needlework classes. They caught on rapidly to the next step, converting their drawings into appliquéd fabric cut-outs. Then they went to quilting technique. Each girl took a square of fabric the size of their paper drawings, and put to work what they'd learned in *Centre* classes, what they'd learned from Jeanne, and what they'd discovered on their own. The completed squares, with their appliquéd designs and fancy embroidery stitches, they fashioned into quilt sandwiches: worked piece over batting over backing square, finished with hand sewn borders. Thirty-five students, thirty-five squares – in less than a week, they had created what would later become *Vie de Lilavois*, the first Haitian quilt.

It was now clear to Jeanne that in order to develop a self-sustaining cooperative, she would first have to encourage the women's creativity, their awareness of what it means to be original. In their dressmaking classes at the *Centre Menager*, following directions exactly was more useful than questioning, exploring, or being original; a pattern is to be followed, a size is precise. For Jeanne and the others who worked with these women, cultivating their creative intelligence would take time and nurturing. For the students, so would learning what these dynamic American lay teachers expected.

Teaching a novel concept – quilts and quilting – and the skills to turn a concept into an object was one enormous leap. Teaching a language which didn't yet exist was another. For Haitians, the native language is Creole, spoken by all. (About ten percent speak French, the second language.) In January 2006, there was no obvious Creole word for "quilt." Jeanne opted for a word currently used in France, *le patchwork*, and then translated to Creole, *fe le patchwok*, "to quilt."

She also recognized that in order to grasp the fundamentals of quilting, the students had to be familiar with certain related mathematical concepts. So Jeanne organized tutorials where several volunteers set out geometric wooden shapes called Pattern Blocks – hexagons, triangles, squares, rectangles, trapezoids, diamonds – and encouraged the *Centre Menager* upper school students to "play" with them. Moving the shapes into patterns awakened in these students a consciousness of the interaction of shapes, showed them the limitless possibilities of pattern designs, freed them from the one-right-answer learning model and, when reshuffled randomly, forced them to be flexible, to think freshly and creatively. For those who worked in pairs or groups, it was also an exercise in problem solving and collaborative learning.

. . .

Jeanne's second trip to Ste. Marie wasn't until January 2007, a full year later. Still unable to find a bona fide quilter, she and three other volunteers took a second crash course. The goal this time was to enlist the cooperation of the faculty of the five *Centres Menager*, assembled there during the Christmas break, and to hold a six-day quilting workshop to teach them skills they could pass on to their students.

The first day, only the sewing teachers showed up. On the second day, teachers of other subjects joined them. As word spread, on day three, yet more came, including Sr. Gibbs. Some cut, others pieced, others stitched, etc. Assembly was done on foot-powered treadle sewing machines. For the women, these skills were basic, the mechanics of quilting, and rapidly learned. But, like their students, there was much in the process that was not typical for them.

Brainstorming, for example. On the first day Jeanne called on her students, all teachers, educated adults, to suggest ideas for a quilt. The women seemed totally mystified. She had brought several large quilts from her collection, along with *Vie de Lilavois*, the student quilt. These she put up on the wall, and pointed out the "theme" of each. She asked the teachers to think of themes of their own. More blank looks. Like their students, they approached the task uncertainly and needed some encouragement. "It was slow going," said Jeanne, but in the end they came up with two pages of ideas.

Vant grangou fè lapriyè dout.

A hungry belly makes a short prayer.

Haitian proverb

Sr. Marie-Françoise Gibbs, head of Les Filles de Marie Reine Immaculée.

Planning advisory team for the formation of the PeaceQuilts cooperatives. (From left to right) Nancy Hibbard, Drack Bonhomme, Sr. Angela Belizai

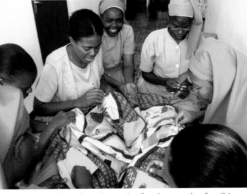

Training school teachers learn the fundamentals of quilting while creating Mon Haiti - My Haiti, shown on page 16.

Undaunted, Jeanne posted the list of ideas on the walls, and gave each teacher six red sticky-dots. Their assignment was for each to cast six votes by sticking her dots next to her favorite themes. One tries to imagine the scene: Two dozen Haitian women, most wearing blue nun's habits, stare at six red American dots. Sr. Angela peels her six off the paper, places one on each finger of her left hand, one on her right thumb. Sr. Marie Nicole covers her mouth with her hand. Sr. Fernand walks to the posted lists and reads them silently. Sr. Angela starts to laugh, raises her dotted hands in the air, waves them from side to side like a fan at a baseball game. Finally, Sr. Rosemane boldly affixes a red dot next to "School days." Sr. Fernand thumbs a red dot next to "Work" and another next to "Food." Sr. Angela asks if she can put all her dots next to one idea. Soon the walls are magnets of activity. In the end, the most dots go to "A Haitian village." They have chosen a theme.

One teacher stood out immediately: Sr. Angela. She was skilled and fast, and had the instincts of a quilter. Before long she was teaching other teachers, the group's acknowledged leader. At the end of the third day, the teachers had pieced the quilt top. The next day they layered and began to quilt it. On the final day they added and hand-stitched the binding and mitered the corners.

On Saturday evening, piles of fabric, needles, embroidery thread, large and small scissors, and other quilting necessaries were left in the workroom at the *Centre* in Port-au-Prince. Sunday was a holy day; there would be no more teaching. After Mass, the volunteers packed to leave, bought carved stone figures from a visiting artisan, and conferred with Sr. Gibbs about the next visit to the *Centre at College Ste. Marie.* The Sisters, still in their dress white robes, headed for the quilting room and quilted until there was no more light. While they gathered for a late supper, Sr. Rosemane brought Jeanne and her companions the first-ever quilt the nuns had been working on, finished.

"Thank you," she said, "thank you for what you have done for us."

. . .

Jeanne returned to Haiti alone in May 2007. On this trip she brought with her no quilting supplies, no fifty-pound suitcases filled with fabric. Her purpose was administrative, and tightly focused. She wanted to return with a structure for a quilting cooperative, one designed to function in Haiti. In order to arrive at an appropriate model, she flew to Jeremie, a town northwest of Port-au-Prince, to meet with three people who understood Haiti and Haitians.

One was an American missionary who came to Haiti speaking no French, who had been working nearby for over three years, and who had learned fluent Creole. Another was Sr. Angela, acknowledged not only for her superior needlework and quilting aptitude, but for knowing how to run a sewing program. A third was a young Haitian graduate student, enlisted for his political savvy, his sensitivity to what makes Haitians different from Americans. By the end of the long weekend, the four were satisfied with the model they'd put together, a design flexible enough to change should the need for change appear.

Jeanne also left with an unexpected gift. Her first night on this trip, at the College Ste. Marie, Sr. Gibbs brought her a stack of quilted squares made by students from outlying schools, students who had

Mon Haiti (My Haiti), November 2008
Teachers and Sisters of Les Filles de Marie Reine
Immaculée; Appliquéd and pieced cottons with
embroidered details, 49 ½ x 50 ½ in.

Anpil men, chay pa lou.

Many hands make a lighter load.

Haitian proverb

Pati bonè pa di kont;
se konnen wout la ki konte.

Starting early
isn't enough;
knowing the
way is what
counts.

Haitian proverb

learned from teachers who attended the January workshop. Sr. Angela gave her a pile of squares which she had done on her own; Sr. Marianne added a few of hers. What Jeanne had hoped for, but had not dared expect, had happened. Teachers and students were making quilts on their own.

· · ·

Over the summer of 2007, another wished-for gift dropped into Jeanne's life. At a fund-raiser on Martha's Vineyard a friend introduced Jeanne to Maureen Matthews McClintock, a psychiatric social worker in Bennington, Vermont, and a master quilter. By the end of the evening, Maureen was making plans to go to Haiti with Jeanne on her next trip. By the end of the evening, Maureen and her

A charcoal filled iron and brazier are part of the low-tech equipment used in the absence of electricity.

Cooking class at the Centre Menager in Lilavois.

Several blocks in Vie de Lilavois that were not completely finished at the first workshop were brought back with Staples to the United States, where a group of quilters at the Oak Bluffs Senior Center in Martha's Vineyard, Massachusetts finished what little remained, and then joined the blocks together. Glenna Barkan (far left) and members of the group.

Women of the cooperative sort fabrics which have been donated by American quilting groups.

Women of Artisanat Patchwork de Paix and PeaceQuilts. (left to right) Ermilienne Désir, Jeanne Staples, Fabiola Marcel, Marielle Loge, Noémie Estimé, Denise Estava, Maureen Matthews McClintock, Nadège Florian, Jo Van Loo (seated)

Kote fil fini se la kouti fini.

Where the thread ends is where the sewing stops.

Haitian proverb

husband Lon McClintock had become committed to the PeaceQuilts project, and would later join its Board. Over the next weeks Lon emailed their entire address list, described Maureen's plans and asked everyone on it to contribute $10 for quilting supplies. In one month they received $1400.

For weeks Lon and their two sons, then eighteen and twenty-one, starched and ironed the fabrics. By November, enough fabric and supplies to fill ten fifty-pound suitcases had been contributed by quilters from all over New England. And thus it was that ten volunteers (including a number who were there for the Fish Farm project) and five hundred pounds of quilting supplies were picked up and hoisted onto a pickup at the Port-au-Prince airport, and unloaded at Lilavois. The next day work would begin.

The next day no work began. The email, which had been sent weeks before asking the teachers to select six of their best sewing students, had not been received. However, once the Sisters realized the importance of a core team, *un equipe*, they set about lining up their best. On the third day, they had agreed on five: Noémie, Marielle, Nadège, and Fabiola, due to graduate in a few weeks, and Denise who had trained at the Centre, but had not completed her studies due to illness. One girl, Annis, who was not selected, slipped in uninvited. The official sixth, Ermilienne, was chosen considerably later.

They got right to work. "They did exactly what they were told to do," Maureen said of the women. "And they were very good." They were deft with needles and pins, but they'd never seen a rotary cutter, razor-sharp wheels which slice straight lines through fabrics and can take off a thumb-tip. They learned quickly to close the cutters between uses, but they did not yet understand the concept of being original. Jeanne and Maureen had to help them cultivate ideas.

They were also shy to the point of reverential. Maureen engaged them, got them working together choosing colors and fabric, and watched as their anxiety eased. Before long, as they chatted, trading

Denise Estava working on l'Arche de Noé (Noah's Arc) and the women of Artisanat Patchwork de Paix.

Shop and dwelling - Lilavois, Haiti

ideas and scissors, they realized that working together was fun. They liked each other. They liked the idea of being a team so much they chose a name for the group: *L'Artisanat Patchwork de Paix.* "Once they got it, they started to be excited," said Maureen. It was magical.

· · ·

As the women became accustomed to working as a team, they began to make decisions independently. The source of water for the classrooms was a pipe and spigot in the children's playground. Rather than make the hot, dusty climb down from the second floor and back every time they needed to wash their hands, the women bought plastic buckets and soap. They didn't have a towel, so someone quilted one out of fabric scraps. They implemented a sun-sterilization setup to purify the bottled water for drinking, and bought cups which they personalized with each quilter's name. When presented with shelving for quilting supplies, they organized the fabric and equipment for maximum accessibility. They designed and installed a roll-up tarp to keep the contents clean. For the next set of shelves, they had the carpenter add sliding glass doors.

All the while, they continued to assume decisions about quilting designs – motifs, colors, size. Frequently they stayed at the workroom long past closing time because finishing a quilt was more important than getting home. In the spring of 2009 Denise couldn't come in to work because of a debilitating case of anemia. While house-bound she started and finished an entire quilt. Nadège, intelligent and dedicated, had been appointed manager. During the summer break she began making home visits to each woman, looking in on their living situations, and providing help and encouragement as needed. No one had asked her to do this; she simply decided it would be beneficial to the

Wòch nan dlo pa konnen doulè wòch nan solèy.

The stone in the stream knows not the pain of the stone in the sun.

Haitian proverb

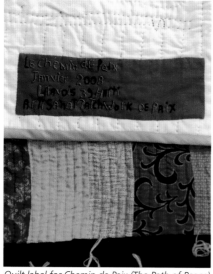

Quilt label for Chemin de Paix (The Path of Peace)

Eder Previlon, Rénand Domi and Milou Jean-Charles, three unofficial members of the cooperative at Lilvaois, work on a quilt.

Ranje Kabann ou Avan Domi Nen Je-w (Make Your Bed Before You Get Sleepy) Detail

Lexpwa fè viv.

Hope gives life.

Haitian proverb

women and to the cooperative. When the women decided to dress alike, in bright red tee-shirts and blue denim skirts, their pride in themselves sang out: "We're a team! We're a brand!"

On subsequent trips to Lilavois, Maureen and Jeanne found the cooperative humming with cheerful industry. From the moment Nadège unlocks the door to the storeroom, the women are at work. First they sweep the floors, briskly moving desks and tables out of the way. Next they mop. A film of red dust has settled on every surface over night, so Ermilienne takes a rag to the wheels and shiny black bodies of the three sewing machines. Fabiola dusts tables and chairs and schoolroom desks. On the balcony, Denise layers charcoal in the brazier and sets it alight. After a while, she will scoop the glowing coals into the iron, a metal cage with jaws like an animal trap.

When the housekeeping is complete, fabrics and color-coordinated bags of spooled thread tumble onto the large worktable. Scissors, packets of pins, tape measures, and masking tape occupy one corner. On the table the women cut, depending on the design at hand, shapes, strips, or squares of fabric. Someone will assemble them on the sewing machines, rapidly rocking heel and toe on the treadle, setting the wheels and vertical stitcher in motion. If a quilt has been assembled, the women will form a circle of desks and sit, facing inward, the quilt on their laps like a communal blanket, and they will thread needles with embroidery floss and sew. They talk, they joke, they sing.

· · ·

Pupils at College Marie Reine Immaculée in Lilavois. While co-op members quilt upstairs, their children can attend school in classrooms below.

Kay koule twanpe soley men li pa ka twanpe lapli.

A leaky roof fools the sun but can't fool the rain.

Haitian proverb

As for their quilts, the year 2008 saw a trickle become a flow. In April, Denise completed "Noah's Ark." Eder, one of the three farm hands who live and work at Lilavois, had finished his quilt which he embellished with buttons. The women started the ambitious collaborative Tree of Life quilt. That summer Sr. Cadet mailed Jeanne fourteen quilts, including the completed "Tree of Life." By the summer of 2009, the PeaceQuilts cooperative had produced over one hundred hand-stitched Haitian

The women begin the formation of the cooperative with workshops taught by Maureen Matthews McClintock.

Nadège Florian pieces a quilt by means of a foot-powered treadle sewing machine.

Eder Previlon works on his quilt La Nuit et la Journée (Night and Day).

PeaceQuilts founder Jeanne Staples and Sr. Angela Belizaire, in charge of student quilting curriculum for PeaceQuilts.

Mon Haiti (My Haiti) detail

Lè pye bwa jwe ak van, li pèdi fèy li.

When the tree plays with the wind, it loses its leaves.

Haitian proverb

Fabiola Marcel (right) in front of her house, pictured with her mother, children and other members of her extended family.

quilts, ranging in size from 20" by 20" to one that would cover a king-size bed. The reputation of these quilts continues to expand with every suitcase brought back from Haiti.

As *l'Artisanat Patchwork de Paix* heads toward self-sufficiency and takes steps toward independence from the sheltering *Centre Menager*, it is tempting to be optimistic about their role as pioneers in a new women-centered industry. Aware that Haiti is known as "the graveyard of projects" because of its instability and lack of resources, visionaries like Jeanne and Maureen tend to temper their optimism. The women at Lilavois are indeed the founding generation of PeaceQuilts, and the project does not stop with them. A new wave of students is mastering *le patchwork* at Lilavois and at other Centres. The original group are not only quilting, but are training to become teachers and founders of *artisanats* elsewhere in Haiti. Partnerships with organizations other than the *Centres* could significantly increase work opportunities for generations of women.

With the opening of the PeaceQuilts exhibition at the Bennington Museum, an art book devoted to the Quilts of Haiti realizes the original vision. Nadège Florian's lively "Disobedience of Jonah," portrays a wild-eyed Jonah half-disappearing into the maw of a charging whale, his arms outstretched in terror. The tight whorls of tiny stitching on in the churning sea remind the viewer of the chaotic skies in Vincent Van Gogh's "Starry Night." More modest, a small twenty-inch square depicting a Haitian *tambou* (Creole for Drum) charms with its simplicity of subject. The Quilts of Haiti radiate art.

• • •

THE QUILTERS
THEIR QUILTS

&

Nadège Florian

From the moment she arrives at the *artisanat* every morning at 7:30 Nadège Florian is at work. She is the first to start sweeping the floor, the first wipe the red dust which has coated the treadle sewing machines and tables overnight, the one who unlocks the storage room and sets out stacks of fabric, the one who lays out the scissors, the bags of color-sorted thread spools, the rulers and pins. Recently she took on another task, and begins each workday by collecting her fellow quilters' cell phones in a basket. No one minds. It has long been accepted that Nadège is in charge.

Elsewhere, at another time, Nadège would be on a fast track to an MBA, but not now, not in Haiti. She lives in Cite Soleil, Port-au-Prince's notoriou slum city, with her mother and four brothers. Her morning commute is arduous, requiring three separate *taptaps* and more than an hour to reach the school. One of her brothers was shot to death during in the Cite Soleil violence in 2008. Her remaining brothers sell lottery tickets; these brothers underwrote her tuition at the *Centre Menager,* where she finished first in her class. Nadège was the first candidate selected for PeaceQuilts.

Out of this grim and difficult setting has come a woman not only of focus but of wide-ranging vision. She quilts beautifully. Her mag icent *Dezobeysans de Jonas* she began and co pleted in her small home in *Cité Soleil.* She ha also begun to draw, to work out on paper wha she will need to create an entirely new design. She wants the world to see what Haiti is like, t show people doing what they do, working, pl ing soccer, doing laundry, carrying babies. She wants to bring Haiti to life in her quilts.

"I think a lot before I come up with a de sign. It's not only the design, but the colors, t fabrics, what pieces are necessary to create tha design," she says. "But it's the colors – they are the most important. I think longest beforehand about the colors."

She loves the cooperative, "every day tha come here." And she is a leader, not only as m ager of the coop's daily routines, but artisticall One day a couple of the quilters started to sing Others joined in. Without a signal, Nadège stoc up, left the circle of sewers, and stood beside sewing machine as if it were a grand piano. Th group paused, and she continued, taking up th solo part in a clear, nuanced soprano. When it was over, she rejoined the circle and took up h needle. Six women continued to quilt, hummi softly.

Dezobeysans Jonas (The Disobedience of Jonah), started July 7, 2008, completed May 29, 2009 in Cité Soleil
  Nadège Florian
  Appliquéd and pieced cottons with embroidered details, 55 x 54 in.

Denise Estava

What does a happy *Haitienne* look like? She looks very much like Denise.

And with good reason. Denise is tall, slender, model-pretty and dresses with the flair of a student of la couture, which she studied at the *Centre Menager*. One week before her twenty-first birthday in January 2009, she became engaged to the boyfriend she grew up with in *Cornillon-Grand-Bois* – she bashfully offers her ringed left hand as evidence.

Both she and Jean-Julles have jobs – a rare situation in Haiti – he as an auto mechanic repairing trucks. Denise has two jobs, rarer still. Mornings she cuts, pieces, and sews with her colleagues at PeaceQuilts; after lunch she joins Sr. Angela to teach sewing to the young women at the Centre, the same program of which she is a recent alum.

Life wasn't always this golden for Denise. "Life in Haiti is difficult," she says. She had finished her fourth level of schooling when a political coup changed her family's circumstances, and there was no longer money for school. She is one of nine children, two of whom go school. Three are at home, unemployed.

Help came when Sr. Irma, head of the *Centre Menager,* called, inviting Denise to wo for PeaceQuilts. She hesitated to accept, for at the time she was responsible for looking after eight-year-old brother Hulrick whom the fami couldn't afford to send to school. Recognizing a precious offer, Denise joined PeaceQuilts, b had to leave the boy with whomever she coul find to look after him. It was a long day for bo of them.

In 2008 one of the American volunteers visiting Lilavois heard Denise's story, and imm diately arranged to sponsor Hulrick's educatio He started school in January 2009.

This spring Denise was diagnosed with severe anemia, and needed to miss a month w PeaceQuilts. In spite of her fragility, she began and finished *La Beauté de la Nature* while rec perating at home,

"It's been difficult, but now I'm happy," she says. "I love the *artisanat* because we wo together. We sew, we cut the fabric with music we use the treadle machine. I love that. I love design the patterns." Her *l'Arche de Noé* is her proof.

"I'm proud of myself." She seems surprise to hear herself say this.

l'Arche de Noé (Noah's Ark), completed April 2008
  Denise Estava
  Appliquéd and pieced cottons with embroidered details, 39 x 47 in.

Fabiola Marcel

Fabiola Marcel lives in Lilavois, a quiet town, with a few grand houses ringed by trees and iron fences, and a lot of little houses on scant squares of red earth. Compared to the hustle and noise, the sharp hills and rutted roads, the cheek-by-jowl quarters of Port-au-Prince, Lilavois is a tranquil suburb. It is here that the Peace-Quilts workrooms are situated. Down these red dirt roads Fabiola walks to work each morning, holding the hand of her four-year-old daughter. Neika, in her pink beads and uniform, goes to the pre-school at Lilavois, one stair-flight down from where her mother works.

Lilavois is a sanctuary for Fabiola and her children. She and her sister were raised in Cité Soleil, Port-au-Prince's vast slum notorious for its trash-littered alleys, its lack of plumbing and schools, its foul odor, and its gangs, which until a few years ago were armed, violent, and in control.

"Life was much harder in Cité Soleil," she says, in clear, precise French. "There's no work there, and it's really dangerous."

Now she shares a house with her three children, her mother, her sister and her sister's child. Her husband left in 2008. Her two older children, Steven who's nine, and Neika, go to school. The baby Rebecca is cared for by her mother and sister. Her sister cannot find work. Fabiola is twenty-nine years old.

Work, and the money it brings, are subjects Fabiola returns to frequently. She is gripped by frustration that her income alone must feed, clothe and educate her three children, and support three additional family members. Fortunately, she's a skilled and devoted quilter. Fabiola would like to make enough money one day to build a little house, just for herself and her children. She would also like to be sure her children finish their schooling. She'd like her son to be a doctor, an engineer, a lawyer.

"He's very intelligent, the best in his class." Her frustration shows. "It's hard to think of the future because we have to think about today. Or maybe tomorrow, at most."

"Life is better for me now than before," she says, "because I'm earning money and, with every quilt I make, have the possibility of earning more." Then a big smile brightens her remarkably pretty face. "I like what I'm doing."

Tomorrow, and each day she'll walk to work holding Neika's hand, paint a future of which Fabiola, not long ago, did not dare dream.

Le Chemin de Paix (The Path of Peace), completed January 2008
  Nadége Florian, Denise Estavat, Noémie Estime, Fabiola Marcel, Anis Kattia, Loge Marielle
  Pieced cottons, 77 x 71 in.

Marielle Loge

Marielle's story is Haiti's dream.

In a country where more than two-thirds of those who want to work do not have formal or lasting employment, Marielle Loge has held a steady job since she was in her teens. On the recommendation of Sr. Irma, she was hired by a Haitian-American couple to cook their meals and clean their house. In return, they paid her tuition at the *Centre Menager.* She was particularly talented at needlework.

After she was selected for the PeaceQuilts team, she learned an entirely new set of skills, and fell in love with quilting. At school she had excelled at *couture,* the design and fabrication of women's clothing. As a member of *l'equipe,* she has discovered new fabrics, to be cut in new ways, to be joined with other fabrics in designs that had never before existed. She loves the textures of quilting fabrics, the shapes she cuts out of them, the meticulous work of piecing one to another to another, into a larger pattern. She finds especially exciting the jewel colors of embroidery floss.

"J'aime l'orange," she says, in French. "I love the color orange."

Marielle's story is also a Haitian reality. Marielle's mother and father are deceased, her father in 2002, her mother in 2004. She has fou brothers and three sisters. None can find work. Of eight siblings, she is the only one employed at two jobs. Not only does she have work now she is able to look to the future. For most Haitians, a career – a planned progression of steps in one's working life – is inconceivable. But Marielle is looking ahead.

"I should like to expand the co-op," she says, her pecan-colored eyes looking thoughtful, "because there are a lot of people who hav no possibility of work." She pauses, rapt in this thought. "It is my dream to set up other *artisan ats,*" she continues. "I should like to be in charg of one, one day."

It is not solely the prospect of employmen that fuels Marielle's ambition. It is also the process, what happens as the quilts are created. Si women design a quilt. Six women, sitting knee to knee, stitch together the pieces, embroider designs, fold the binding, and together hold up the final composition.

"When a quilt is finished, I am really proud," she says.

Lap Péché Pwason (Fisherman), started August 15, 2008, completed May 13, 2009
  Marielle Loge
  Appliquéd and pieced cottons with embroidered details, 38 ½ x 38 ½ in.

Sister Angela Belizaire

With all five of her solo quilts in the Bennington Museum exhibition, and six on which she collaborated with students or fellow teachers, Sister Angela is the reigning Queen of Quilts. One of her earliest is *The Tree of Life quilt*, for which she designed the eponymous tree (her students are responsible for the fish border); a recent one is *Deye Mon Gen Mon* ("Beyond Mountains There Are Mountains"). Another bears the name of a wise Creole proverb: *Kay Koule Twonpe Soley Men Li Pa Ka Twonpe Lapli*, ("A Leaky Roof Fools the Sun but Can't Fool the Rain."). Some she quilted with members of the *artisanat*, another quilt she designed was completed by two needlework students. Indeed, Sr. Angela is the resident inspiration and daily guidance behind the vibrant art of PeaceQuilts.

"Me, I love quilting," she says.

Not for herself, she insists, but "for the women, so later they can earn a living with it. I prepare samples. I sew as well. I cut the fabric. Then I show them how to do it." She makes teaching sound simple, but as she talks about it, her rich contralto soars up the scale in enthusiasm.

She is also the Queen of Exuberance. How many home economics teachers, making the rounds of her classroom, chuckle, erupt into scales of room-filling laughter, sashay around the scattered desks, hips gyrating, hands clapping, all because something a student has done utterly delights her? Sr. Angela does.

Sr. Angela works hard, every day, including Sunday. At the *Centre Menager* in Lilavois

she teaches not only needlework but *la coutu* (dressmaking) and *la cuisine* (cooking). She oversees other schools in the town of Lilavois She plays the drums (*le tambour*) at the Roma Catholic services in town. She tends the vege bles and herbs in the farm's hand-tilled garde until dark obscures them, cooks all meals ove charcoal brazier, and bakes pastries in a crank oven. The wellbeing of three resident sisters, and their frequent guests, depends largely on Angela.

To do the Lord's work is something Ang Belizaire wanted from the time she was six ye old. She grew up in Cabaret, a small town in t northwest of Haiti, with three sisters and two brothers. She first petitioned to become a nov when she was seventeen, but was told she wa too young, that she had not finished learning what she needed before making such a comm ment. Already an accomplished seamstress, sh taught sewing and embroidery from her home She finished school on a scholarship in *coutu* and, thanks to the generosity of an American sponsor, in 2005 went on to study *haute couture*. Despite several interruptions from health problems, she graduated, on time and first in class.

The order of the Daughters of Mary Que Immaculate of Haiti was founded in 1971 by a Catholic sister who had been raised and well educated in the orphanage of the Sisters of St. Joseph. Upon graduating, Elda St. Louis entere their novitiate, and went on to teach there for twenty years. During this time she witnessed countless young girls for whom there were no schools sell themselves on the street to make a living. She vowed to establish a shelter for the children. After more than twelve years being rebuffed by the church hierarchy, Sr. Elda, fifty five years old, and young Sr. Gibbs, now the head of the *Centre* at Ste. Marie in Port-au-Prin received permission to found the order of *Les Filles de Reine Marie Immaculée d'Haiti*. Sr. E became Mother Monique.

l'Alphabet (Alphabet), completed January 2008
  Sr. Angela Belizaire
  Appliquéd and pieced cottons with embroidered details, 39 x 67 in.

In a large house rented for them by the local Bishop the two Sisters began to take in girls of the street as well as girls who'd been orphaned or abandoned. Here the model for the *Centres Menagers* at Lilavois and Ste. Marie was created. This order admitted the honors graduate Angela Belizaire, and set her about doing her life's work as Sr. Angela. Like the first teachers thirty-eight years ago Sr. Angela is teaching poor young women how to cook and sew, training them in the skills that will turn them into valued housekeepers for wealthy families, or skilled workers for Haiti's hospitals and factories, should prosperity every return.

Sr. Angela is a teacher of quilting, and an excellent one. But quilting means more than a curriculum item to her. After the quilters go home, after the *Centre* students leave for the day, the beans are picked, dinner is cooked and records updated, Sr. Angela returns to her fabrics, picks up her needle, and quilts. In the fading light of early dusk, she pieces and bastes vibrant squares. Tiny, precisely spaced stitches merge the layers together. She sings, sometimes hymns, sometimes folk tunes. She is quiet and serene. Her quilts are beautiful.

"*Moi, j'aime faire le patchwork,*" she says.

When Sr. Angela loves, she loves with her whole being.

Noémie Estimé

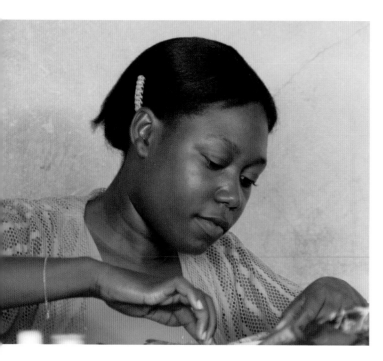

If the life stories of the PeaceQuilt craftswomen appear to be variations on a similar theme, the theme from which their tunes derive belongs to Noémie Estimé.

"I live with my family: my mother, my three brothers, my two sisters," she says. "My mother does not work. My father, who does not live with us, also cannot find work. My grandmother lives next door. My family is poor, and life is hard. I am the only one who has a job."

Perhaps the role Noemie's income plays in her family's wellbeing comes across more loudly, more distinctly, than that of the others. At age 25, she not only feeds and clothes seven people in addition to herself, she pays for her younger brother's schooling. "My family is poor, and life is hard" is not so much a complaint as it is an assessment of the way life is in Haiti, a summing up of the plight of everyone she knows.

Every source of data about Haiti agrees: Haiti is the poorest country in the Western Hemisphere. An estimated eighty percent of its people live below the poverty line. Average annual income, based on Gross Domestic Product, is $1200. Factory jobs pay $2 per day for an eight-hour day; most people live on less than that. In

this context, Noemie's daily wage for a five-day looks sumptuous; it supports a family of seven. She and the others are also are paid a commission on every quilt they make, plus a additional sum when the quilt is sold; four exhibition quilts have come to life under he gers. That she can also help educate her bro is something she is grateful for.

"My dream is to help my family," she s "I stay in the afternoon to help Sr. Angela in sewing course. That way I can pay my broth tuition."

Noemie realizes that her brother's and own education stand out as rarities. One rep table estimate puts Haiti's literacy rate at 53% Less than 15 percent of Haitian children age to eleven are enrolled in public school, one the lowest rates in the world. Non-public scl cost more than $100 per year, and families w can afford to pay private tuition costs one ye frequently cannot in subsequent years. Most tian children do not make it to sixth grade. S are teenagers by the time they do.

"At the *Centre Menager* we had course cooking and sewing, but we also had mathe ics and languages," Noemie reflects. "I loved sewing best."

PeaceQuilts' theme reflects hard times, it is played up-tempo, in a major key.

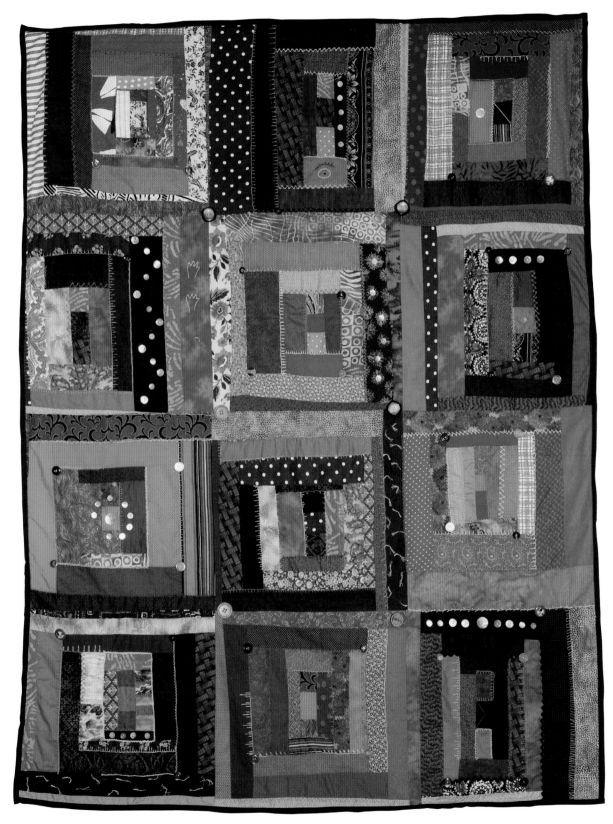

Piti Piti (Little by Little), started February 13, completed March 13, 2009
   Nadège Florian, Noémie Estimé, Denise Estava, Ermilienne Désir, Marielle Loge, Fabiola Marcel
   Pieced cottons with embroidered details and applied buttons, 62 x 47 in.

Sr. Rosemane Alice

In appearance, Sr. Rosemane is all angles. Her cheekbones are high and sharply contoured. Her shoulders are wide and slender, like over-grown coat-hangers. Her arms and legs remind one of a grasshopper, or a teenager whose coordination has not yet caught up with her growth spurts. Yet set her to dancing and she is all fluid grace, clapping, sidling, swaying to drummed rhythm. To see her walk is like watching water ambulate.

For several years a teacher of sewing at the Lilavois *Centre Menager*, Sr. Rosemane is as graceful with a needle as she is in motion. She says she first learned to sew from her mother, a couturier and seamstress who did "extraordinary" embroidery. Her skills grew further in school, in courses very similar to those she teaches at Lilavois. But quilting was new to her, and she took to it.

"We knew how to sew here, we knew how to make all kinds of things," she says, a tone of wonder coloring her unhurried, precise French. "Now we have learned something new, something very different from what we'd done before."

What they'd done before was classic mo − human figures, palm trees, animals − finely embroidered on cotton table cloths and napki There once was a thriving market for the Siste needlework, but in the current no-iron culture sales have dried up like water in a noonday puddle. With the advent of PeaceQuilts, Sr. Rc mane found new roads to explore with her sk

"*J'imagine, et puis je le fait*," she says. "*J'aime la couleur, surtout des couleurs vives, couleurs animées.*" I love color. Above all I lc strong colors, lively colors.

"*J'aime des belles choses aussi.*"

Perhaps her creativity, her love of color, and her appreciation of what is beautiful in life were the motivations for Sr. Rosemane's choos ing a life in service to the Church. For a woma skilled in the domestic arts, there are in Haiti f avenues of employment. Sr. Rosemane viewec her future with a perspective more profound than job availability.

"I chose the Church because it gave me t opportunity to make something special of my life," she reflects.

Indeed, Sr. Rosemane has the opportunity to more than most Haitian women. She runs the farm at Lilavois, overseeing the care of the pig the chickens and the goats. She raises her food and will never go hungry. She teaches young women to become employable. She lives in a community of strong and merry women, and will never know isolation. If she becomes ill, s will be cared for. She designs and sews beauti quilts. She sings and she dances.

"*J'aime la vie quand même*," she says. "I love this life," a wide smile sculpting new plan among the angles of her face.

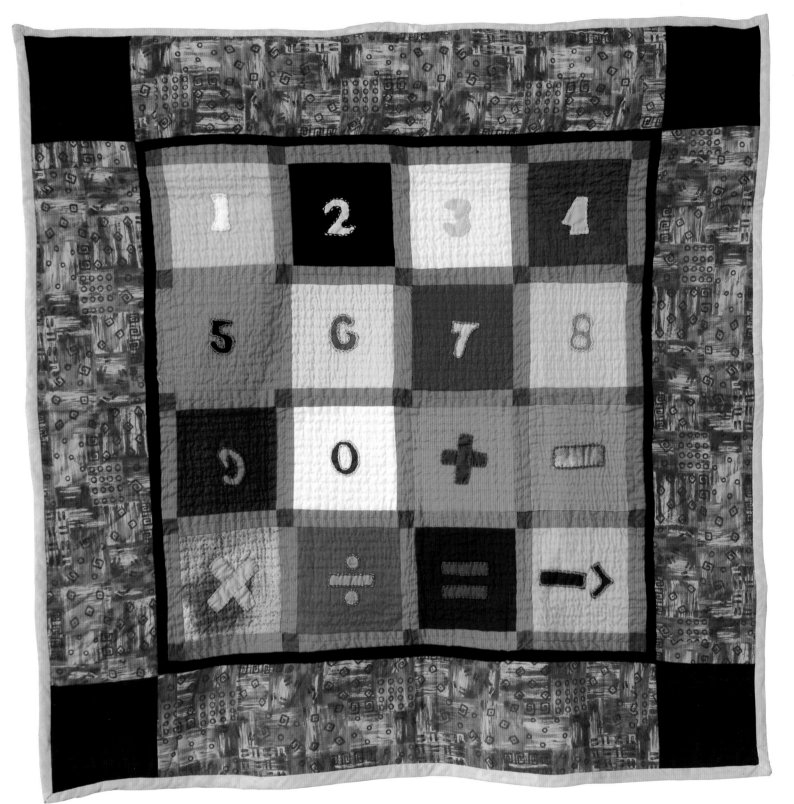

Edem Grandi (Help Me Grow), completed March 2008
  Sr. Rosemane Alice.
  Appliquéd and pieced cottons with embroidered details, 32 x 32 in. From the collection of Marston and Louise Clough.

Martha's Vineyard Watercolor by Susan

Ermilienne Désir

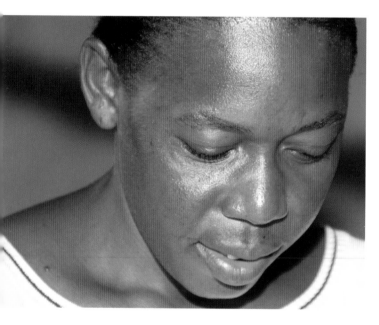

The island of La Gonave, in the bay off Port-au-Prince, was Ermilienne Désir's childhood home. Life there was difficult for a little girl, with mile-long treks to fetch water from mountain springs. Farmers on the rural island till small plots of eroded land, its soil washed to the sea because the hills have been cleared of trees to make charcoal for fuel. Staples, such as rice, beans and plantains are scarce, therefore expensive. Jobs are hard to come by, and those who have them often find themselves supporting brothers, cousins and aunts in addition to their immediate families.

Ermilienne is one such woman. She and her five-year-old son, Givenghi Guerschom Lahens, share a house in Lilavois with her aunt, her cousin and her cousin's two sons. Her cousin leaves early to look for work. Her aunt is not well. Her son's father helps out occasionally, but given the reality that eighty percent of children in Haiti are

not acknowledged by their fathers, Ermilienne does not count on his support. So she and her son set off eagerly for school every morning, to kindergarten, she – breadwinner for six – to the *artisanat* at Lilavois to rejoin the sisterhood of quilters.

Having a son is hard, Ermilienne confess her soft voice hesitant and low. "I must educate him. I'd like him to become a doctor." She knows from her own life that her son's education is his way out of poverty. She left La Gonave for Lilavois where she attended L'Ecole de Sainte Therese de l'Enfant Jesus until she was twenty two. Mostly without work during the years that followed, she was thirty-three when she started at the *Centre Menager*, hoping to acquire skills work as a domestic or a dressmaker.

At 38, she is the oldest of the quilters. Completing the courses at the *Centre Menager* gain her not only mastery of needlework, but entry into a team of artisans and a new world of design and ideas. She loves quilting, has pictures in her mind of quilts she'd like to work on. "*Dessins plus sophistiques, fines, raffines,*" she says, a note of boldness in her voice. New ideas she'd share with her fellow quilters, so together they could explore designs for quilts more sophisticated a they've done so far.

"I dream of living in a more tranquil place with friends, where you can count on having food available," and being able to send her son to school without disruption.

"If God grants it, it will happen," she says reluctant to share the credit.

Ombre Pete Lumière (Shadows of Light), October 2008
Nadége Florian, Denise Estavat, Noémie Estime, Fabiola Marcel, Anis Kattia, Loge Marielle, Ermilienne Desir
Pieced cottons, 97 x 79 in.

Tout Bagay pou Bondye (All Things for God), completed May 2009
  Designed by Sr. Angela Belizaire, quilted by her students
  Appliquéd and pieced cottons with embroidered details, 63 x 63 in.

La Nuit et la Journée (Night and Day), completed April 2008
  Eder Previlon, pieced by Denise Estava
  Appliquéd and pieced cottons with embroidered details and applied buttons, 47 x 38 in.

Machann Fwi (Fruit Vendor), completed May 2009
  Rose-Marie Agnant (student)
  Appliquéd and pieced cottons with embroidered details, 35 x 29 ½ in.

Kay Koule Twonpe Soley Men Li Pa Ka Twonpe Lapli (A Leaky Roof Fools the Sun But Can't Fool the Rain), February 2009
  Sr. Angela Belizaire
  Appliquéd and pieced cottons with embroidered details, 40 x 45 ½ in.

l'Arbre de Pomme (Apple Tree), completed May 2007
  Sr. Manouse
  Appliquéd cottons with embroidered details, 20 x 21 in. From the collection of Leanne Emerton.

l'Arbre de Vie (Tree of Life), completed May 2008
   Sr. Angela Belizaire and Nadège Florian, Denise Estavat, Noémie Estimé, Fabiola Marcel, Anis Kattia, Loge Marielle, Ermelienne Desir
   Appliquéd and pieced cottons with embroidered details, 51 x 53 in. From the collection of Richard and Marney Toole.

Vie de Lilavois (Lilavois Life), begun January 2006 and finished January 2008
Students of Centre Menager, Lilavois
Appliquéd and pieced cottons with embroidered details, 49 ½ x 40 ½ in.

Mon Haiti (My Haiti), November 2008
  Teachers and Sisters of Les Filles de Marie Reine Immaculée
  Appliquéd and pieced cottons with embroidered details, 49 ½ x 50 ½ in.

Dèyè mon gen mon (Beyond Mountains there are Mountains), completed April 2009
    Sr. Angela Belizaire
    Appliquéd and pieced cottons with embroidered details, 48 x 55 in.

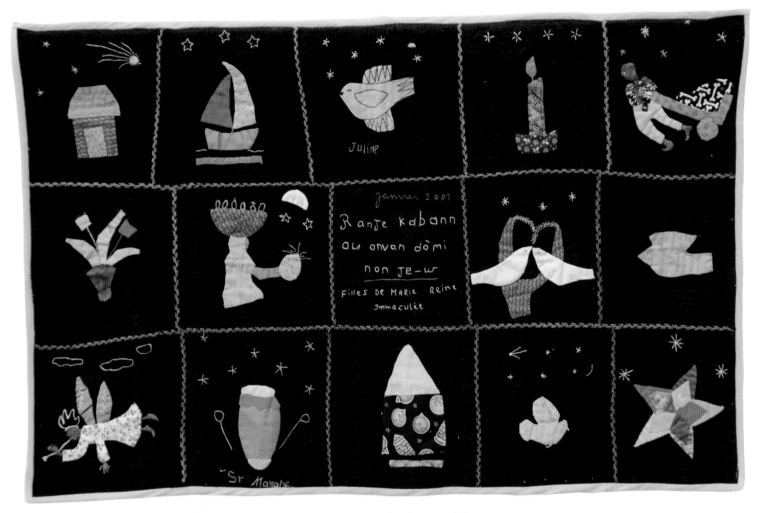

Ranje Kabann ou Avan Domi Nen Je-w (Make Your Bed Before You Get Sleepy), completed January 2007
  Teachers and Sisters of Les Filles de Marie Reine Immaculée
  Appliquéd and pieced cottons with embroidered details, 26 x 40 in.

Sa ou genyen, Se li ou Pote nan maché (What You Have is What You Bring to the Marketplace), completed March 2009
 Sr. Angela Belizaire, quilted by students Ruth et Myrlaine
 Appliquéd and pieced cottons with embroidered details, 41 x 42 ½ in.

Fan-tastique, completed May 2008
  Sr. Angela Belizaire and Students of Latiboliere
  Pieced cottons with embroidered details, 58 x 58 in.

La Vie Haïtienne (Haitian Life), completed May 2007
  Sr. Angela Belizaire
  Appliquéd and pieced cottons with embroidered details, 48 x 51 in.

Toute la Création (All of Creation), completed May 2008
  Anis Kattia
  Appliquéd cottons with embroidered details, 45 x 73 in.

SELECTED BIBLIOGRAPHY

PA PALE SA OU PA WE AK PROP ZYE OU.
Never talk about anything you don't see with your own eye

Bank, Mirra. 1995. *Anonymous Was a Woman: A Celebration in Words and Images of Traditional American Art a the Women Who Made It.* New York: St. Martin's Griffin.

Dance, Daryl Cumber, ed. 2002. *From MY People: 400 Years of African American Folklore.* New York and London: W. W. Norton & Company.

Desmangles, Leslie G. 1992. *Caribbean Art.* London: Thames and Hudson.

Grudin, Eva Ungar. 1990. *Stitching Memories: African-American Story Quilts.* Williamstown: Williams College Museum of Art

Phillips, Ruth B. and Christopher B. Steiner, ed. 1999. *Unpacking Culture: Art and Commodity in Colonial and Postcolonial Worlds.* Berkeley, Los Angeles and London: University of California Press.

Picton, John. 1999. *The Art of African Textiles: Technology, Tradition and Lurex.* London: Barbican Art Gallery in association with Barbican Art Gallery.

Poupeye, Veerle. 1998. *The Faces of the Gods: Vodou and Roman Catholicism in Haiti.* Chapel Hill and London: Tl University of North Carolina Press.

Rodman, Selden. 1988. *Where Art is Joy, Haitian Art: The First Forty Years.* New York: Ruggles de Latour.

Stebich, Ute. 1992. *A Haitian Celebration: Art and Culture.* Milwaukee: Milwaukee Art Museum.

Stebich, Ute. 1978. *Haitian Art.* Brooklyn: The Brooklyn Museum.

Turnbull, Wally R. 2005. *Hidden Meanings, Truth and Secret in Haiti's Creole Proverbs.* Durham: Light Messages.

Wahlman, Maude Southwell. 1993. *Signs and Symbols: African Images in African-American Quilts.* New York: Stue Books in association with Museum of American Folk Art.

SA OU PLANTE SE SA OU REKOLTE.
What you plant is what you harvest.

BOOKS

Turnbull, Wally R. *Creole Made Easy.* Durham, N.C.: Light Messages, 2008.

_____ *Hidden Meanings, Truth and Secret in Haiti's Creole Proverbs.* Durham, N.C.: Light Messages, 2005.

The Quilts of Gee's Bend. Atlanta, GA: Tinwood Books, 2002.

NEWSLETTERS, PROGRAMS, PAMPHLETS

Charpentier, Lorrie. Translation, from *Constitution of the Congregation*, Background of Mother Monique, Sister Eld St. Louis, Foundress of the Daughters of Mary Queen Immaculate of Haiti. (undated).

Haitian Art Sale Benefit. Program, Seventh Annual: Martha's Vineyard Fish Farm for Haiti Project, July 18, 2009.

Hibbard, Nancy. Newsletter: "April 2009 Haiti Update (Healthcare as I see it)," May 01, 2009.

Martha's Vineyard Fish Farm for Haiti Project. Newsletter, Winter 2008.

Women Artists of Matenwa, Haiti, The. Release: *RaRa Gallery*, Wellfleet, MA. July 01, 2009;

SPEECHES

Lassegue, Hon. Marie Laurence Jocelyn. Speech, Chilmark Library, July 16, 2009.

_____. Speech, Haitian Art Sale Benefit, Martha's Vineyard Fish Farm for Haiti Project, July 18, 2009.

NEWSPAPERS, TELEVISION

Boston Globe, The. "Deadly food crisis grips Haiti," Jonathan Katz, November 23, 2008.

_____ "Haiti's ongoing disaster," Donna J. Barry and Kimberly Cullen, November 24, 2008

_____ "US implored to stop deporting Haitians; Protected status urged for battered country," Marcia Sacchetti, May 13, 2009, A12.

Boston Globe, The (online). "'The Agronomist' is a labor of love" (movie review), Ty Burr, April 30, 2004.

CNN.com. "'Misery breeds violence' in Haiti's seaside slum," Claire Doole. May 23, 2009.

New York Times, The (online). "Living in a Sea of Mud, and Drowning in Dread," Neil MacFarquhar, March 24, 2009.

_____ "A Boy Living in a Car," Nicholas D. Kristof, March 29, 2009.

_____ "Haiti's Big Chance," Ban Ki-Moon, March 31, 2009.

_____ "Haitians in U.S. Illegally Look for Signs of a Deporting Reprieve," Kirk Semple, May 28, 2009.

¬¬¬¬¬¬¬_____ "9 Die as Haitian Immigrants' Boat Sinks," Damien Cave, May 14, 2009.

WEBSITES

http://countrystudies.us/haiti/19.htm. *Haiti.* "Geography."

http://diplopundit.blogspot.com/2009/06/officially-in-kenneth-h-merten-to-port.html. June 5, 2009.

http://geology.com/world/haiti-satellite-image.shtml. *Haiti Map.*

http://haiti.usembassy.gov/speech_.html. "Ambassador Janet A. Sanderson – American Chamber of Commerce Farewell Dinner in Honor of the Ambassador," June 9, 2009.

http://haiti.usembassy.gov/warden_information.html. July 12, 2009.

http://ipsnews.net/print.asp?idnews+34657. *Haiti: Exhausted School System Gets a Second Chance*, Amy Bracken, May 08, 2009.

http://movies.nytimes.com/movie/review. *FILM REVIEW; Elegy for the Unflinching Conscience of Haiti*, "The Agronomist," April 23, 2004.

http://travel.state.gov/travel/cis_pa_tw/tw/tw_917.html# *Haiti.* January 28, 2009.

www.alterpresse.org/spip.php?article4046. *Haiti's Public Schools* (Debate), Ericq Pierre, January 30, 2006.

www.haitipeacequilts.org.

www.infoplease.com/ipa/A0107612.html. *Haiti.* "Geography," "Government," "History,"

www.lonelyplanet.com. *Haiti.* "Religion," "Arts," "Environment," "Vodou."

www.museeacadien.ca/ *Exposition et Vente de Courte Pointes – Quilt Expo and Sale*, July 22, 23, 24, 2009.

www.state.gov/g/tip/rls/tiprpt/2006/65991.htm. *Haiti.* "Trafficking in Persons Report 2006."

www.state.gov/secretary/rm/2009a/04/121674.htm. *Remarks at the Haiti Donors Conference*, Hilary Rodham Clinton, April 14, 2009.

www.state.gov/secretary/rm/2009a/04/121829.htm. *Remarks at Interamerican Woven Garment Factory*, Hilary Rodham Clinton, April 16, 2009.

www.williambowles.info/haiti-news/2005/sanderson.html. "Who is Janet Sanderson, Haiti US ambassador nominee?" Lyn Duff, November 23, 2005.

. · · ·

CREDITS

STEPHEN PERKINS – *Executive Director, Bennington Museum*

Since 2001, Stephen served first as Curator and now Executive Director of the museum. A graduate of the prestigious Winterthur Museum/University of Delaware program in Early American Culture, he has worked to make the museum relevant to Vermont, and the nearby regions of New York and Massachusetts by expanding access and programming as part of the museum's strategic goals. Under his direction, the museum has mounted a mix of innovative local exhibitions and high-visibility traveling shows to provide a compelling visitor experience.

JAMIE FRANKLIN – *Curator of Collections, Bennington Museum*

Jamie Franklin has developed a distinguished reputation for planning, researching, and implementing exhibitions from the permanent collection, traveling exhibitions, and temporary loan shows. His extensive experience includes working for the Philadelphia Museum of Art, the Clark Art Institute, the Smithsonian American Art Museum, and the Williams College Museum of Art. He has written for various publications and lectures widely.

NORA MACFARLANE NEVIN – *Writer*

Nora Macfarlane Nevin has lived in the Republic of Ivory Coast, Japan, and New Zealand. She now lives, writes and entertains on Martha's Vineyard. She was staff writer for Scholastic Magazines and the Miami Herald, and taught non-fiction writing at the University of New Hampshire. She has degrees from Wellesley College and UNH. She wishes everyone could have the good fortune to visit Haiti.

HARVEY JOHN BETH – *Photographer*
Winner of over two dozen awards in photography, Harvey Beth's work has been published in numerous magazines, publications and annual reports. Educated at the Maine School of Photography, he has exhibited in galleries and art shows throughout New England. He is or has been the professional photographer for several Martha's Vineyard agencies including the American Cancer Society's Relay for Life, the MV Cancer Support Group, the Island Community Chorus, the Island Housing Trust, Habitat for Humanity and the Dukes County Housing Authority. He has also taught courses in developing, dark room techniques, working with color saturated films and business development for artists. He has traveled extensively, taking photographs in Africa, South Africa, New Zealand, Australia, China, Tibet, Egypt, France, England, Scotland, Wales, South America, Central America, Canada, Mexico and through out the United States.

JEANNE STAPLES – *PeaceQuilts founder and Director*
Jeanne Staples has spent her entire professional career working in the arts. In addition to being the founder and Director of Peacequilts, she serves on its Board of Directors, and previously served on the board of the Martha's Vineyard Fish Farm for Haiti Project. Since completing her studies at the Pennsylvania Academy of the Fine Arts, she has worked continuously as a professional artist. In addition, she has served as Coordinator of Education for The Empire State Plaza Art Collection and the New York State Governor's Mansion; adjunct instructor at the College of St. Rose in Albany, New York; and instructor of painting and drawing at The Albany Institute of History and Art. She now lives and works on Martha's Vineyard, and is represented by galleries in Edgartown, MA, Boston and Windham, NY.

MAUREEN MATTHEWS MCCLINTOCK – *PeaceQuilts Quilting Coordinator*
Under Maureen's direction, not only have the PeaceQuilts cooperatives received intensive training on quilting techniques and work protocols, she has been involved in formulating and directing all facets of the PeaceQuilts project, and serves on the board of directors. She is a practicing psychotherapist for the Veteran's Administration Outpatient Clinic in Bennington, Vermont, and maintains a private psychotherapy practice. Her past service includes serving as president of the Board of Directors for the Project Against Violent Encounters, and as president of the North Bennington Graded School Prudential Committee. She has traveled to Haiti, the Solomon Islands, Australia, New Zealand, Canada, Costa Rica, the Dominican Republic, Curacao, the U. S. Virgin Islands, Bermuda, Ireland, Spain, and Germany.

ACKNOWLEDGEMENTS

PeaceQuilts thanks the following for their generous support and contributions to the Bennington Museum Exhibition and the PeaceQuilts initiative in Haiti.

Haiti: Sr. Marie-Françoise Gibbs, Sr. Irma Corriélus, Sr. Angela Belizaire, Sr. Rosemane Alice and the nuns and students of *Les Filles de Marie Reine Immaculée of Haiti*; Marie Laurence Jocelyn-Lassegue – Minister of Women's Affairs & Gender Issues for Haiti; Ann-Valerie Timothee Milfort; Ellen LeBow and the women artists of Matènwa, Haiti; Drack Bonhomme; and Claude Winddcheley Saturné.

The Bennington Museum: Steve Perkins, Executive Director, assisted with design and execution of the exhibition and served as a guiding light behind the project. Jamie Franklin, Curator of Collections, guided PeaceQuilts in its preparation for the traveling exhibition and coordinated the work of the Museum staff; Susan Strano, Marketing Coordinator, made sure people know about the exhibit and organized a very festive opening; Tom Moriarty, Building & Grounds Manager, oversaw the fabrication of installation materials and prepped the gallery; Deana Mallory, Director of Public Programs, coordinated all public programs related to the exhibit; Joy Danila, Development Associate, secured funds, sponsorships, and/or grants used to mount the exhibition; Callie Stewart, Collections Manager, coordinated all the registrarial duties, including shipping, insurance, loans, etc.; Greg Van Houten, Proprietor of GVH Studio (of Bennington), fabricated exhibition labels; L & G Fabricators (of Bennington), fabricated brackets for the quilt installation. Karen Harrington, Visitor Services Manager, coordinating representation of PeaceQuilts products at the Museum Gift Shop.

PeaceQuilts Volunteers & Supporters: Kristina Almquist; Eric Anderson; Glenna Barkan and the Oak Bluffs Senior Center quilters; Bennington Rotary Club; Lynne Benson; Ellie Beth; Rev. Dr. Judith Campbell; Dr. Alix Cantave; Nancy Davies; Dave & Shirley Dayton; Dawn Dayton & Peter King; Patricia Dean; Liz Devlin; Leanne Emerton; Karen Flynn; the Honorable Linda Dorcena Forry; Rev. Dr. Jerry Fritz and the Edgartown Federated Church; Rhonda Galpern; Haitian Outreach and Child Sponsorships of Leominster, MA; Nancy Hibbard; Jill Iscol; Jacobs, McClintock, & Scanlon, LPC; Julie Jaffe; Douglas Jones; Judy Kniffin, Sheila Mullineaux and the Unitarian Universalist Fellowship; Joseph Kira; Jan & Russ Leslie; Barbara MacIntyre and the Peace Resource Center; Barbara Maggio; Tania Magloire; Betsy Marshall; the volunteers of the Martha's Vineyard Fish Farm for Haiti Project; George & Kathy Matthews; Carter McClintock; Edie McClintock; Lon McClintock; Matthew McClintock; Todd & Cathy McClintock; Dave & Carol Newell; The New England Quilt Museum; Margaret Pénicaud and the Board of Little Children of Mary; The Quiet Valley Quilt Guild; Andrea Quigley; Ursula Slavick; Margaret Spokus; the Honorable Marie St. Fleur; Shirley Thomas and First Mountain Design; Marney & Richard Toole; Taylor Toole; Ann Valérie; Jo Van Loo; Tomar Waldman; Ed & Stacey Whitten; and the YaYas. Jeanne Staples would particularly like to thank Margaret Pénicaud and the volunteers of the Martha's Vineyard Fish Farm for Haiti project for the support and encouragement which gave PeaceQuilts its start.

In addition, we would like to thank the many quilters, guilds, clubs, and organizations that have generously contributed their interest and support, including materials, supplies, equipment, and money. We are certain to have inadvertently left out some names from the list above, but your contributions have been important and our appreciation is heartfelt. The good will and encouragement of all has proved infectious and invaluable.

Bebe ("Baby")
completed January 2008
Ermilienne Désir
72 x 52 in.

La Beauté de la Nature
("The Beauty of Nature")
completed March 2009
Denise Estava
72 x 72 in.

Esperans ("Hope")
completed March 2009
Milou Jean-Charles and
Rénand Domi
58 x 58 in.